JACK THE LAD

A Musical Celebration

by David Wood and
Dave and Toni Arthur

SAMUEL FRENCH

Copyright © 1991 David Wood and Dave and Toni Arthur
All Rights Reserved

JACK THE LAD is fully protected under the copyright laws of the British Commonwealth, including Canada, the United States of America, and all other countries of the Copyright Union. All rights, including professional and amateur stage productions, recitation, lecturing, public reading, motion picture, radio broadcasting, television, online/digital production, and the rights of translation into foreign languages are strictly reserved.

ISBN 978-0-573-01801-5

concordtheatricals.co.uk
concordtheatricals.com

FOR AMATEUR PRODUCTION ENQUIRIES

UNITED KINGDOM AND WORLD
EXCLUDING NORTH AMERICA
licensing@concordtheatricals.co.uk
020-7054-7298

Each title is subject to availability from Concord Theatricals, depending upon country of performance.

CAUTION: Professional and amateur producers are hereby warned that *JACK THE LAD* is subject to a licensing fee. The purchase, renting, lending or use of this book does not constitute a licence to perform this title(s), which licence must be obtained from the appropriate agent prior to any performance. Performance of this title(s) without a licence is a violation of copyright law and may subject the producer and/or presenter of such performances to penalties. Both amateurs and professionals considering a production are strongly advised to apply to the appropriate agent before starting rehearsals, advertising, or booking a theatre. A licensing fee must be paid whether the title is presented for charity or gain and whether or not admission is charged.

This work is published by Samuel French, an imprint of Concord Theatricals Ltd.

The Professional Rights in this play are controlled by David Arthur, Silver Birches 31 Brian Crescent, Tunbridge Wells, TN4 OAN, David Wood c/o Casarotto Ramsay & Associates Limited, 3rd Floor, 7 Savoy Court, Strand, London, WC2R 0EX, Toni Arthur-Hay Manor Farm Barns Northwold West End, IP26 5LE.

No one shall make any changes in this title for the purpose of production. No part of this book may be reproduced, stored in a retrieval system, scanned, uploaded, or transmitted in any form, by any means, now known or yet to be invented, including mechanical, electronic, digital, photocopying, recording, videotaping, or otherwise, without the prior written permission of the publisher. No one shall share this title, or part of this title, to any social media or file hosting websites.

The moral right of David Wood and Dave and Toni Arthur to be identified as author of this work has been asserted in accordance with Section 77 of the Copyright, Designs and Patents Act 1988.

USE OF COPYRIGHTED THIRD-PARTY MATERIALS

Licensees are solely responsible for obtaining formal written permission from copyright owners to use copyrighted third-party materials (e.g., artworks, logos) in the performance of this play and are strongly cautioned to do so. If no such permission is obtained by the licensee, then the licensee must use only original materials that the licensee owns and controls. Licensees are solely responsible and liable for clearances of all third-party copyrighted materials, and shall indemnify the copyright owners of the play(s) and their licensing agent, Concord Theatricals Ltd., against any costs, expenses, losses and liabilities arising from the use of such copyrighted third-party materials by licensees.

USE OF COPYRIGHTED MUSIC

A licence issued by Concord Theatricals to perform this play does not include permission to use the incidental music specified in this publication. In the United Kingdom: Where the place of performance is already licensed by the PERFORMING RIGHT SOCIETY (PRS) a return of the music used must be made to them. If the place of performance is not so licensed then application should be made to PRS for Music (www.prsformusic.com). A separate and additional licence from PHONOGRAPHIC PERFORMANCE LTD (www.ppluk.com) may be needed whenever commercial recordings are used. Outside the United Kingdom: Please contact the appropriate music licensing authority in your territory for the rights to any incidental music.

IMPORTANT BILLING AND CREDIT REQUIREMENTS

If you have obtained performance rights to this title, please refer to your licensing agreement for important billing and credit requirements.

JACK THE LAD

Commissioned by the Library Theatre Company, the play was first presented by the City of Manchester Cultural Services at the Library Theatre, Manchester, on 23rd March, 1984, with the following cast of characters:

Jack	David Scase
Nelson	Frank Elliott
Maria	Cynthia Grenville
Zeldy	Sophia Winter
Rose	Myra Sands
Tom	Ric Morgan
Young Jack	Howard Ward
Frank	Jeremy Swift
Reuben	Rod Arthur
Betsy	Michelle Fine
Darren	Sheldon Robinson
	Nigel Murphy
Charlotte	Lindsey Ashworth
	Claire Billingham
Jason	Jason Pollitt
	Jason Shaw
Dog	Bess

Director   Roger Haines
Musical Director   Simon Lowe
Choreography   Jean Newlove
Designer   Jenny King
Lighting Designer   Tim Wratten
Sound   Michael Williams

CHARACTERS

All are members of various branches of a gypsy family.

Jack	eighty years old, the elder of the family
Nelson	Jack's son, fiftyish
Maria (pronounced Mar*y*a)	Jack's daughter-in-law; Nelson's wife, fortyish
Zeldy	Jack's granddaughter; Nelson and Maria's daughter, twentyish
Rose	Jack's daughter, forties
Tom	Jack's son-in-law; Rose's husband, forties
Young Jack	Jack's grandson; Rose and Tom's son, twenties
Frank	Jack's grandson; Rose and Tom's son, twenties
Reuben	Jack's sister Alice's son, mid thirties
Betsy	Reuben's wife, mid thirties; Scottish*
Darren **Charlotte** **Jason**	Reuben and Betsy's young children
Bess	Nelson's lurcher dog

The action of the play takes place in a gypsy encampment

Time—the present

*(See Production Note on page vi)

INTRODUCTION

Jack the Lad is a musical celebration of Jack, the ubiquitous hero or everyman of English legend, myth and folklore; from Little Jack Horner, through Jack and the Beanstalk to Spring Heeled Jack, the Terror of London.

The setting is a gypsy encampment, and the Jack tales and songs are performed by the gypsies to celebrate the eightieth birthday of their senior member—affectionately known to the family as Jack the Lad. Although the play depicts contemporary gypsy family life, as well as traditional gypsy customs and superstitions it is not a sociological play about gypsies.

It is important that the actors playing the gypsy family find a balance between truthfully playing each family member acting in a Jack tale and using their actors' skills to enhance the characterization. In other words, sometimes fun will be gained from a gypsy not being equipped to play a certain role in a Jack tale, but such moments should not be over-indulged. Every member of the gypsy family is, for the purposes of the play, a good actor!

The show uses a basic set—a gypsy encampment in the countryside, with an attractive wagon plus a flat wagon to act as an occasional platform. All props and extra costumes would be on stage, in or out of the wagon. The gypsies should appear to improvise telling their stories, so that simplicity and inventiveness of presentation is the key.

Apart from the show musicians, it is hoped that some of the cast will be able to play the simple basic gypsy instruments, like the melodeon and the mouth-organ, or the penny whistle. Jack himself, who does *not* play all the Jacks in the show, but is our focus, because it is his eightieth birthday and the other gypsies are paying their tribute, should be a fiddler. Naturally, the actor might have to mime playing the fiddle.

The musical depicts various gypsy skills, such as stepdancing—a simple form of tap-dancing. Other traditional dances will also be employed. Plus occasional acrobatics, puppetry, and story-telling.

A variety of theatre techniques will be employed also within the main framework, including a mumming play, stories narrated with accompanying mimed action, a shadow-mime, plus vocal and dancing skills.

In the script we have often indicated which gypsy character might best play which parts in the Jack tales. But occasionally we have left this to the director. In the narrated tales, it is suggested that several actors can share the narration; this spreads the load and also helps drive the story forward.

The action of the musical takes place in the evening. Night draws on as the show progresses.

David Wood and Dave and Toni Arthur

PRODUCTION NOTES

Betsy. If no member of the cast can produce an authentic Scottish accent then Betsy can be played as a Southern English gypsy. Drop any references to Scotland and anglicize Betsy's lines. Her mouth music (Music No. 6) would then be:

> Derby, Derby, won't you marry me?
> Derby, Derby, won't you say yes?
> Derby, Derby, won't you marry me?
> Show your legs to the Cock-er-ney gels.
> Doo dee doo dee doo dee diddle dee
> Doo dee doo dee diddle dee doo
> Doo dee doo dee doo dee diddle dee
> Show your legs to the Cock-er-ney gels.

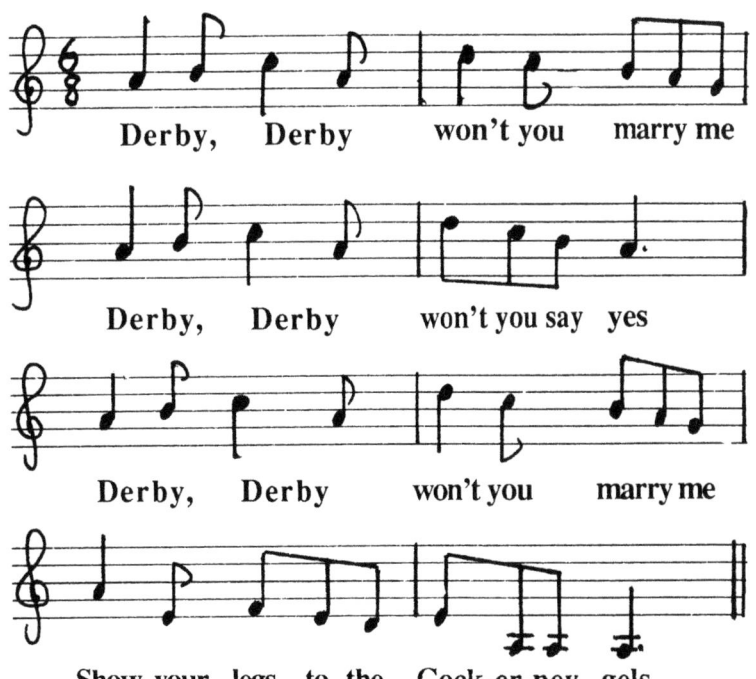

Spring Heeled Jack. Some productions have just used the Spring Heeled Jack song (Music No. 9) to top-and-tail the story and not incorporated it into the story action.

Information on step-dancing and Broom Dances can be obtained from the Vaughan Williams Memorial Library, English Folk Dance and Song Society, Cecil Sharp House, 2 Regents Park Road, London NW1 7AY. Telephone 071-284 0523.

MUSICAL NUMBERS

ACT I

No. 1	Page 1
No. 2	Page 2
No. 3	Page 3
No. 4	Page 4
No. 5	Page 8
No. 6	Page 8
No. 7	Page 9
No. 8	Page 9
No. 9	Page 15
No. 9A	Page 18
No. 10	Page 18
No. 10A	Page 19
No. 10B	Page 19
No. 11	Page 19
No. 11A	Page 21
No. 11B	Page 21
No. 11C	Page 21
No. 12 Entr'acte	Page 22

ACT II

No. 13	Page 22
No. 14	Page 23
No. 15	Page 25
No. 16	Page 28
No. 16A	Page 29
No. 17	Page 30
No. 18	Page 31
No. 19	Page 33
No. 19A	Page 35
No. 19B	Page 37
No. 19C	Page 37
No. 19D	Page 39
No. 19E	Page 39
No. 20	Page 40
No. 21	Page 40
No. 22	Page 40
No. 23	Page 42
No. 24	Page 44

Musical Numbers

No. 25..................................Page 44
No. 26..................................Page 45
No. 27..................................Page 46

The vocal score is published separately by Samuel French Ltd

Musical Plays by David Wood and Dave and Toni Arthur
The Pied Piper
Robin Hood

ACT I

A gypsy encampment in the open air. Evening

A gypsy wagon, a flat wagon to act as an occasional "stage", a large box containing costumes and props, and a washing line with a large sheet hanging on it. A camp fire downstage

Silence, as the Lights come up

No. 1

A fiddle is heard off stage playing a minor version of "Jack of All Trades" **Music**

Jack enters, playing the fiddle. As the tune stops, he sits down on the steps outside his wagon, leans back to hang his fiddle on the wall of his wagon and then sits forward, with his head on his hands. All this sequence is evocative of loneliness

After a short silence, the fiddle music starts again, in the distance. Jack reacts

Nelson (*off; singing*) He's a roving Jack of all trades,
Of every trade and all trades,
And if you want to know his name,
They call him Jack of all trades.

Nelson enters

He's travelled wide the countryside,

Others join in the song off stage, then enter

He's rambled round the nation;
He's not too grand, he'll turn his hand
To any occupation.

The whole company have arrived. Jack is bemused and delighted. The song is directed at him

All	He's a roving Jack of all trades,
	Of every trade and all trades,
	And if you want to know his name,
	They call him Jack of all trades.
Tom	He can set a snare to trap a hare,
	He says there's nothing to it,
Reuben	Or show a mare at Barnet Fair;
	He knows just how to do it.
Frank	He can train a dog or split a log,

Music	**Young Jack**	Or thatch a barn with heather,
	All	And if you chance to see him dance,
		He's lighter than a feather.
	(*Dancing about*)	He's a roving Jack of all trades,
		Of every trade and all trades,
		And if you want to know his name,
		They call him Jack of all trades.
	Maria	He can catch a trout or fix the spout
		Of your old copper kettle;
	Zeldy	He's a real dab hand with pots and pans
		And any kind of metal;
	Betsy	He can read your palm or spin a yarn,
	Rose	Or make a heather basket,
	All	And if you want to hear a song,
		You've only got to ask it.
	(*Dancing about*)	He's a roving Jack of all trades,
		Of every trade and all trades,
		And if you want to know his name,
		They call him Jack of all trades.
		He's travelled wide the countryside,
		He's rambled round the nation;
		He's not too grand, he'll turn his hand
		To any occupation.

The music ends. All face Jack

Jack Bugger me! What a turn-out! What's all this for?
All Happy birthday, Dad/Grandad!
Jack God bless you! (*He sings*)

Music   **No. 2**

>   I'm a roving Jack of all trades,
>   Of every trade and all trades,
>   And if you want to know my name,
>   They call me ...

He encourages the others

All   ... Jack of all trades!
Jack (*speaking*) Cor, I wish my Lucy could see this.
    (*Singing colla voce*) I took a wife to share my life,
>   And never did regret it;
>   As bride and groom, we jumped the broom;
>   Oh, how could I forget it?

Act I

> I love her still, I always will, **Music**
> An angel and a dragon;

Soft laughter from the others

> The laughs and tears of forty years
> Still echo round this wagon.

All (*standing still this time*)
> He's a roving Jack of all trades,
> Of every trade and all trades,
> And if you want to know his name,
> They call him Jack of all trades.

The family present gifts to Jack

Nelson
Maria } (*together*) Happy Birthday, Dad.

Rose
Tom } (*together*) Just a little something to show you're not forgotten, Dad.

Zeldy Have a lovely time, Grandad.

Frank Happy Birthday, Grandad.

Young Jack Here y'are, Pops.

Reuben Great to see you looking so well.

Betsy Ay—ye've still that wee sassy look about ye, Uncle Jack.

Children Happy Birthday, Great Grandad.

Nelson (*thumping the box to get attention*) Right now, all together.

They all sing "Happy Birthday". Then, cheers and merriment. The family start to sit down. Nelson stands with his thumbs stuck in his braces

No. 3 **Music**

(*Singing*)
> We've come along to sing a song,
> A song of Celebration,
> For Jack whose light has shone as bright
> As any constellation.
>
> We'll shed no tears for passing years,
> Let no-one here be sad;
> So join us all, both great and small,
> And sing for Jack the Lad.

All
> For he's a roving Jack of all Trades,
> Of every trade and all trades,
> And if you want to know his name,
> They call him Jack of all trades.

Cheers and excited chat. Nelson interrupts

Nelson (*still in MC-type pose, thumping again on the box*) Come on now, settle down. (*Looking at Maria particularly*) You can gossip later on.

All settle

Right now. (*He clears his throat*) We have come here today to pay our respects to one of the finest members of our family. And we've gathered as many of us as was able to get here from all over the country.

As each member of the family is announced he or she acknowledges it with suitable gesture

There's your Rose and her Tom all the way from Norfolk, with their Frank—who's come here special-like from his university in Sussex, and might I say we're all very proud of him!

Clapping

And, of course, their other son, Young Jack, your namesake, Dad—sorry about the 'aircut. Your sister Alice's son, Reuben, and his wife, Betsy, all the way from Scotland—och ay the noo! And their three little 'uns, Darren, Charlotte and young Jason. Me wife Maria, me daughter Zeldy, and, of course, meself, your son, Nelson. Well, I think that's about it. Now——

Rose What about Bess?

Nelson What d'you mean, what about Bess?

Rose Well, you can't leave her out, Nel. She's part of the family too.

Nelson Ah all right, don't go on, woman. (*Back to MC voice*) H'and of course our old lurcher Bess, what Dad gave to me seven years ago. God bless 'er. Course she's getting a bit grey round the nose now, but she can still pick up a rabbit or two. Can't you? You're a good old girl. Right now, where was I? Ah yes—Dad, we thought we'd have a little party for you to celebrate the last eighty years. There's been many a Jack before you, Dad, but as far as we're concerned you're the best Jack of them all. Jack Woods, everyone, the original Jack the lad.

All cheer. Young Jack starts to wave a Union Jack and music starts up again

No. 4

Music **Tom** (*jumping up, singing*)
There's Union Jack and Jumping Jack

Young Jack jumps up and does a flick-flack

Reuben
And even young Jack Horner;
There's Jack the Slipper and Jack the Ripper
Lurking round the corner;

Young Jack There's Spring Heeled Jack and Gypsy Jack,
The champion of the ring;

(*He mimes boxing actions*)

Darren
Charlotte } (*together*) There's Jack and Jill ... But I tell you still

Act I

Nelson   That Jack the Lad's the king.   **Music**

All   He's a roving Jack of all trades,
Of every trade and all trades,
And if you want to know his name,
They call him Jack of all trades.

Frank (*standing and singing colla voce*)
Now Jack's a name of noble fame,
In song and rhyme and story.

Reuben (*interrupting*) That's it Frank, go on, you tell 'em.

Frank (*undeterred*)   Jack Ketch, Jack Spratt who'd eat no fat,
Jack Frost and *Jackanory*.

Rose He's a clever boy.

Frank   There's Jack O'Lent and Jack of Kent
And Jack within the Green;
There's Fiddler Jack …

(*He looks as if out of ideas*)

Children   … and *Crackerjack*.

The music stops as Frank jokingly threatens the children, who run to Betsy, their mother

Betsy (*putting her arms around her children protectively*) And Jack who bought a bean …

The company go straight into the first Jack Tale—"Jack and the Beanstalk". It is narrated by one or more of the company, as required, and acted out by them. Those not "performing" act as an audience

Narrator   As old Mother Twaddle was sweeping her floor
She found a new sixpence under the door.
And as she surveyed it with exquisite pleasure
She called her son,

Mother Twaddle   Jack, come look at my treasure.

I will comb thee and wash thee and make thee quite spruce
Thou shalt go to the fair, to buy me a goose
For of all the good things, I vow and protest
A goose is the nicest and I love it the best.

Narrator   When Old Mother Twaddle had sent Jack to the fair
She hastened with onions and sage to prepare
A stuffing all sav'ry for the delicate treat
And thought,

Mother Twaddle	With what glee those tit-bits I'll eat.
Narrator	Jack got to the fair on the village green.
Trader	Come buy,
Narrator	cried a trader,
Trader	this extraordinary bean. It possesses such virtues that sure as a gun Tomorrow it will grow near as high as the sun.
Narrator	Jack bought it for sixpence, then went to his ma, Who at sight of the bean went white and cried,
Mother Twaddle	Aaaaah!
Narrator	She gave him a flogging and tied both his hands And said,
Mother Twaddle	This'll teach you to mind my commands.
Narrator	Jack went in the garden and took up his spade Then put this rare bean in the hole he had made. He prayed,
Jack	May it grow, a great wonder of wonders As tall as a tree to make up for my blunders.
Narrator	Next morning Jack rose to view this large bean When, surprising to tell, e'en the top was not seen. He made a long ladder of very strong rope And soon mounted on high, full of joy and of hope.
	Jack climbed and he climbed till he ran out of puff He climbed and he climbed, still it weren't far enough. Till just when he thought,
Jack	Phew, I'll never get there.
Narrator	He arrived at a place that hung in mid-air.
	He knock'd at the door of a very grand place A damsel came to it with a cap all of lace.
Damsel	Oh, pray go away,
Narrator	cried this maid in a fright,
Damsel	For a giant lives here and he'll eat you this night.
Narrator	Jack begg'd,
Jack	Let me in,
Narrator	with so winning an air, That she promis'd to help him.
Damsel	Quick hide over there.
Narrator	He'd no sooner hid than the door open'd wide And in stalked the giant with a very long stride.

It is suggested that the Giant be played by one actor on another actor's shoulders

Then the monster roar'd,

Monster	Fe, fi, fo, fum, I smell the blood of an Englishman Be he alive or be he dead, I'll grind his bones to make my bread.
Damsel	Oh wait, my dear Giant, first drink some strong wine, Then on that dainty you may afterwards dine.
Narrator	He seiz'd a large cup and tippled so deep That he tumbled down flat, and fell fast asleep.
	Soon as Jack saw him fall, he crept from the bed, Then snatch'd a large knife and chopt off his head. Thus he killed this great man as he loudly did snore And never again was the giant seen more.
	Jack called to his mother,
Jack	Hey, come up and dine! There's plenty of goose and a bottle of wine.
Narrator	And as she did eat it, with excessive delight She approved of his bargain and said,
Mother Twaddle	You've done right!
Narrator	Jack sent for a parson, as he had a great mind To marry the damsel who was willing and kind.
Parson	I declare,
Narrator	said the parson,
Parson	you're now man and wife.
Narrator	And they lived very happy for the rest of their life.

The performers bow, others cheer and applaud

Nelson Cor, I loved them old tales you used to tell, Dad. Told 'em to me own kids, didn't I?

Jack Your mum couldn't half tell a story, too.

Reuben Yeah. Great day for the gypsies that—when the Woods and the Browns tied the knot.

Betsy I wish I'd met old Lucy.

Jack Ah, Lucy Brown from London Town. Glad I went to Hoxton Market that day.

Maria She was one of the best.

Jack Yeah. Only woman I knew that could sell a three-legged donkey to a jockey.

Laughter. The children start chanting

Children Lucy Brown, Lucy Brown, Lucy Brown, Lucy Brown!

Then music starts, and they dance to their song

Music   **No. 5**

> Oh fernal up and down,
> Jack's gone to London Town
> To marry Lucy Brown;
> He's chased her up and down.

The words are repeated as often as necessary for the dance.

Two children (Darren and Charlotte) take hold of each other's arms, facing each other, or hands placed on each other's shoulders, and dance three steps to each side alternately singing the words as they dance up and down with a swinging movement. Then they swing each other round to the next three bars. This brings them C. *Young Jack and Jason join in the next sequences, leading to the final chorus, by which time everyone should be singing*

All   Oh fernal up and down,
Jack's gone to London Town
To marry Lucy Brown;
He's chased her up and down.

The music stops, but the rhythm continues as Nelson and Jack start to play the spoons as accompaniment to a final dance by the children. Others clap in rhythm. The children stop, and watch the spoon playing; clapping still goes on as in a rhythmic pattern as if the clapping is a thing in itself. Then Betsy starts "mouth music" to go over the clapping (see Production Note on page vi)

No. 6

Music **Betsy**   Brochan loun tannan loun brochan tanna sooie.
Brochan loun tannan loun brochan tanna sooie.
Brochan loun tannan loun brochan tanna sooie.
Brochan loun say tannan loun say brochan tanna sooie.

Brochan loun tannan loun brochan tanna sooie.
Brochan loun tannan loun brochan tanna sooie.
Brochan loun tannan loun brochan tanna sooie.
Brochan loun say tannan loun say brochan tanna sooie.

This is repeated as needed. After a chorus or so, all clap. Betsy continues as Reuben gets up and does some stepdancing, Scottish style. Lots of vocal encouragement. Someone puts sticks on the ground crossed over like swords. Reuben carries on his dance like a sword dance, but knocks the sticks out of line, which makes Frank jeer

Reuben OK. You do better yourself then, you cocky bugger!

A sort of stepdancing competition begins. All applaud each other and comment on each other's performance

Frank OK. I'll have a go. Tune us up a hornpipe, Uncle Nelson.

Act I

No. 7 — Music

Nelson starts to diddle a hornpipe

Rose He's a good dancer he is, he's an all round dancer, he can dance to hornpipes, jigs, breakdowns, or he can dance to the latest style music—anything. Go on, Frankie!

Frank starts to step to Nelson's diddling. Jack picks up his fiddle to help accompany the dance. Onlookers can clap in rhythm and the band could come in one at a time, particularly the drum

Nelson (*to Maria*) Have a go, love!

Maria is next to dance. Then, Young Jack. Then, Nelson. Finally Zeldy dances, but quickly gets puffed and stops. The music cuts out

Jack (*putting down his fiddle*) You young 'uns are all the same—no bloody stamina. (*He walks down from the steps to* C)

No. 8 — Music

(*Singing*)
    Tiddly wink old man,
    Suck a lemon if you can,
    If you can't suck a lemon,
    Suck an old tin can.

    You should never take your daughter
    On a sea trip to Gibraltar,
    If you want to see her marry
    Wiv a nice young man.

Jack starts to dance as the company start to sing the tune or "la la" it. All join him in a line and dance with him. His steps get more complicated and one by one they drop out leaving Jack dancing on his own and finishing with a spectacular flourish. All cheer and applaud Jack. Jack returns to the steps, basking in his applause

Young Jack Right old twinkletoes, isn't he!
Zeldy Fair bit of stepping that!
Jack Yeah! I can still get the old leg up. (*He holds up his leg*)
Frank But can you still get it over, Grandad?
Jack Cheeky bugger! (*He kicks Frank*) Byronic these knees are. Byronic! (*He does another couple of shuffles*)
Nelson Watch out, Dad. You'll be in Australia soon if you go on like that.
Rose I don't know about Australia, but did you hear about Jack Frankam over Kent way? He could dance right through stone.
Jason What's that then?
Rose Haven't you heard that one, our Jason?
Charlotte What is it? Tell us!

Rose Well, once upon a time there was lots of chals and juvas all having a dance just like we was afore. It was evening and they was dancing in the moonlight in front of a great big house. "I wish that house was mine," says young Jack Frankam. Now the gentleman of the house, who was watching the dancing like, comes out of his house like, and says to Jack, "When you dance a hole through the centre of that stone you're standing on, I'll give you the house." So d'you know what Jack did? He made a pair of shoes out of iron—the devil's metal, and danced and danced on that stone till the sparks flew. He danced and he danced and he danced and he danced, and by the morning, sure enough, he'd wore a hole right through the middle of it! So the rich folk had to give him the house. And that's why we says a stone with a hole in it brings good luck.

Reuben Well, everyone knows that. I've got one, I wear it all the time.

Children Give us a look, Uncle. Show us!

Reuben (*taking his hole stone on its thong, from round his neck*) There you are, it's just a stone with a hole in it.

Tom We call them adder stones in our part of the country.

Betsy We call them hag stones. They hang them over the cow byres.

Children What do they do?

Tom What don't they do?

Betsy They stop the witches stealing the cows' milk.

Reuben (*mock threatening*) They keep away the evil eye. And protect you from Old Nick.

Young child 1 Old Nick?

Young child 2 Who's Old Nick?

Young child 1 Is he like Old Bill?

Reuben Worse than Old Bill! The Devil himself! The Beng! It takes a Jack the Lad to get one over on him. Listen.

Reuben starts the narration of the story of "Jack and the Devil"

It is suggested that the Crows be hand puppets, operated by actors and children. The Big Crow (the Devil) should be an actor. The story is narrated and played/mimed

Narrator (Reuben)	On a farmer's field near Hereford town
	The crows were having a ball.
	Stuffing their beaks with the precious grain
	While idle Jack lay snoring;
	His master's toil went down the drain
	'Cos Jack found work so boring.
Farmer	Jack! Wake up, you lazy tyke!
Narrator	The farmer swung his stick.
	Jack yelled and tried to run away
Jack	Sorry, sir, I was tired.
Farmer	If you don't keep them crows at bay,
	I swear, lad, you'll be fired!
Jack	If only,

Act I

Narrator	thought Jack, as the farmer stomped off,
Jack	I could find a foolproof plan
	To scare the crows away for good.
Narrator	Then suddenly he saw
	A giant crow fly from the wood;
	It landed and said,
Crow	Caw!
	Hallo, Jack, you're looking glum.
	I've come to help you out.
Narrator	Jack gasped; he couldn't believe his ears—
Jack	A crow that talks is rum!
Crow	Now, listen, Jack, allay your fears,
	You need a friend—I've come!
	Leave all the other crows to me
	They'll gobble no more grain.
	For I possess amazing powers.
Narrator	All Jack could do was stare.
Crow	Just give me, say, a couple of hours
	While you go to the fair.
Jack	The fair!
Narrator	Jack cried; wide-eyed he sighed
Jack	I've always longed to go.
Crow	Then here's your chance, set off with speed;
	I swear I'm on the level.
Narrator	So off Jack went, not knowing he'd
	Been tempted by—the Devil.

The Crow "exits" cackling

	The fair was full of marvellous things
	Like archery and skittles.
	Jack watched a funny puppet show,
	He clapped a morris dance.
	Then just as it was time to go
	He saw, as if by chance …
	… a tiny tent all painted black
	With silver stars that glittered.
	Outside a man with weathered skin
	Was shouting loud and bold,
Gypsy	Roll up, roll up, folks, come on in
	And have your fortunes told!
Narrator	He drew the curtain, Jack stepped in
	And found a gypsy woman.
	With his last coin he crossed her palm,
	She huddled 'neath her shawl,
	And muttering a magic charm
	Gazed in her crystal ball.

Gypsy Woman	Suddenly she caught her breath; Beware the talking crow! Don't give him what he wants tonight, Be strong and never crack. Believe me, Jack, you'll see I'm right. What's more, he's coming back!
	Throw the dog's bone on the bridge, That's what you have to do.
Narrator	
Jack	Jack thought, This fortune-teller's bent! I've wasted all my money.
Narrator	Annoyed he left the stuffy tent; Outside was bright and sunny.
	But suddenly he felt a hand And heard a voice familiar.
Farmer	You skiving rogue,
Narrator	the farmer cried.
Farmer	Take that! And that!
Narrator	Jack squealed.
Farmer	How dare you take me for a ride! Who's caring for my field?
Jack	A crow, sir,
Narrator	Jack replied, aware His answer sounded silly.
Farmer	A crow?
Narrator	the farmer roared,
Farmer	A crow?
Narrator	And shook the trembling youth.
Jack	Come, sir, please! And I will show You that I speak the truth.
Narrator	They reached the field and sure enough 'Twas empty and untouched.
Jack	You see, I didn't spin a yarn!
Farmer	But where are all the crows?
Narrator	Well, on the rafters in the barn Crows silent sat in rows.
	And one, the largest crow of all Appeared to wink at Jack. The farmer sensed an evil force, Backed frightened through the door, Then hastened home astride his horse And bullied Jack no more.
Jack	Thank you!

Act I   13

Narrator	Jack exclaimed—the crow
	With beady eye replied.
Crow	One good turn deserves another
	As two halves make a whole.
Jack	That's fair,
Narrator	said Jack
Jack	What would you like?
Crow	Dear Jack, I'd like your soul.
Narrator	Then, in a flash, remembered Jack
	The gypsy woman's warning.
Gypsy Woman	Beware, beware the talking crow.
Narrator	Was this what she had feared?
	Jack shook his head and shouted,
Jack	No!
Narrator	The crow just disappeared.
	The years went by and Jack, in time,
	Forgot the whole affair.
	He reached the age of sixty-four,
	Strong and active yet.
	A stranger knocked upon his door,
	And called,
Devil	Hail, Jack, well met!
	I've heard you're good at building things.
Narrator	Jack said,
Jack	That is my trade.
Devil	I have a job for you to do.
Jack	I'm busy, sad to say.
Devil	It's worth a bag of gold to you!
Narrator	Jack said,
Jack	I'll start today!
Narrator	He wanted Jack to build a bridge
	Across the nearby river.
	Jack worked all day without a break,
	The bridge was half complete.
	His ageing bones began to ache,
	He muttered,
Jack	I'm dead beat.
Narrator	The Devil, for that's who it was,
	Thought,
Devil	Now at last I've got 'im.
Narrator	Jack fell asleep and woke to find
	His bridge a heap of rubble.
Devil	Come, start again,
Narrator	the stranger snarled.
Devil	Go to it at the double.

Narrator	The Devil thought the strain would kill him
	But Jack worked bravely on.
	Slowly—though, his strength diminished—
	The bridge was seen to rise.
	Finally the job was finished
	And Jack could claim his prize.
Devil	Congratulations, what fine work,
Narrator	The Devil sneered and then—
Devil	Before I pay you, I implore
	You give my bridge a try ...
Narrator	Then, in his mind, Jack heard once more
	The gypsy woman's cry.
Gypsy Woman	Throw the dog's bone on the bridge,
	That's what you have to do.
Devil	Just cross my bridge to yonder side
	And test each stepping stone.
Narrator	Jack looked around, a dog he spied
	Playing with a bone.
	His life was fading fast and yet
Jack	The Devil must not win.
Narrator	Jack took the bone and threw it
	Across the bridge he feared;
	The poor dog saw him do it—
	Followed—and disappeared ...
	Jack had won; the Devil knew
	He'd really met his match!
Devil	To win Jack's soul is far too hard,
	I'll search some other prey.
Narrator	The moral is, be on your guard,
Jack	Or he'll catch you some day!

The actors bow; the others applaud

Nelson Well, you're all right then, aren't you?

Reuben What do you mean?

Nelson Your hole stone—the Devil won't touch you while you've got that.

Frank Come on now, it's all superstition. That's the trouble with us ...

Rose Now listen, young Frank—you with all your education—it doesn't matter how much you know or how clever you are, you can't beat fact. Luck is luck.

Nelson She's right you know. Look at old Isaac. His horse dropped dead, one of his lungs collapsed, his money got pinched and then his wife ran off with the social worker. Now you can't say all that was chance, my boy.

Tom Right. You know as well as me, my son, Isaac got his just deserts 'cos he didn't keep the law—our law.

Rose I always said bad luck would come of it.

Act I 15

Tom He should have burned his old man's van when he died. But no, not him, greedy bugger. "What's the old ways to me?" he says. "That old van," he says, "'s'worth a mint and I'm not burning all his belongings just to keep up some old superstition," he says.
Rose So he sold the lot didn't he? Even the gold out of the poor old sod's teeth.
Nelson And his Crown Derby—made a pile out of that he did.
Tom Yeah. Right cock o' the north he was for a while—new car, new telly, purple and green plush carpets ...
Rose But he had it coming to him ...
Nelson We could all see it ...
Tom Now he's lost the bloody lot—serves him right.

Murmurs of agreement

(*Forcefully*) When the head of a family dies, his things die with him.

An embarrassed silence. All furtively look at Jack to see if Tom's words have registered

Jack (*after a pause*) Tom's right. They should all be burned with him. Wagon and all. (*Meaningfully*) Right, Nelson?
Nelson Right, Dad.
Frank (*under his breath*) Superstition.
Tom That's enough!
Frank No, no, I don't mean that. It's just that my Jack story for Grandad is all about superstition, the unnatural.
Maria Come on then, son. Let's hear it.
Frank All right. But you've all got to be in it as well—it's like a play. (*From his rucksack he takes out pages of script which he hands round*)
Young Jack What's all this then?
Maria Play acting!
Nelson That's education for you!
Frank Shut up! Shut up! Now listen. I came across this when I was researching the Victorian times. It's the weirdest, most frightening Jack of them all and this one was *real*. (*Formally he announces*) Spring Heeled Jack, the terror of London!

During the story, Frank has to encourage his "cast" to join in. Some find it embarrassing. However, this should not be overplayed; the narrative drive should keep going. All read their parts. See the Production Note on page vi

No. 9 Music

(*Singing*) We'll tell you the tale of Spring Heeled Jack,
He could jump like this,

He indicates to Young Jack to jump

He could jump like that,

He indicates to Reuben to jump

Music

> With claws of steel
> And eyes of fire,
> He could jump as high as the old church spire.
> All the police in London Town
> They couldn't pin him down.

(*Speaking*) February eleventh, eighteen-thirty-eight. Bearbind Lane, Bow, East London. Spring Heeled Jack attacks a young girl, then leaps over a ten foot high wall to make his escape.

All (*singing*)   We'll tell you the tale of Spring Heeled Jack.

Young Jack (*speaking*) Cutthroat Lane, Clapham Common. Spring Heeled Jack jumps over a stile and attacks Mary Stevens, parlourmaid. He tears her clothing, touches her bosom, then leaps cackling into the night.

All (*singing*)   He could jump like this,
                    He could jump like that.

Betsy (*speaking*) Streatham High Road. Carriage almost wrecked as horses run wild, frightened by a huge creature that leapt from the shadows. Injured coachman unable to say whether man or bird or beast.

All (*singing*)   With claws of steel
                    And eyes of fire.

Reuben (*speaking*) Forest Hill. The leaping terror of London town surprises a gent and lady returning from dinner. He slashes the man across the face with his claws, then half-blinds the woman with foul fumes emitting from his lips. Escapes in massive leaps and bounds.

All (*singing*)   He could jump as high as the old church spire.

Frank	Camberwell!
Nelson	Hounslow!
Maria	Peckham Fair!
Tom / **Rose** (*together*)	Spring Heeled Jack is everywhere!
Frank	Richmond!
Zeldy	Lambeth!
Young Jack	Barnes!
Tom	Hyde Park!
Reuben / **Betsy** (*together*)	Everywhere he leaves his mark!
All (*singing*)	All the police in London Town
	They couldn't pin him down.

Frank indicates to Nelson to be a policeman

Nelson (*reading, embarrassed*) Hallo, hallo, hallo, I am a policeman. And I am baffled. We are nowhere near solving this mystery. Take young Jane Alsop.

Frank indicates Betsy to "play" her

Betsy I was on my own at home in Bow. I'd heard the rumours about Spring Heeled Jack, but never taken them seriously. Suddenly——

Frank knocks on the wagon to suggest a door knock

Act I

Who's there? **Music**

Frank indicates to Reuben to start acting

Reuben I'm a police officer.
Nelson (*aside*) I thought *I* was the policeman.
Frank (*aside*) Shut up, Nelson! Go on, Reuben.
Reuben I'm a police officer. For God's sake bring me a light, for we have caught Spring Heeled Jack in the lane.
Betsy The stories are true after all! I'll see him being arrested! (*She takes a candle and mimes opening a door*) Aaaaaah!
Frank (*aside*) Hang on. He hasn't done anything yet! Go on, Reuben.

Reuben clumsily attacks Betsy. The others hiss

Betsy Aaaaaah!

A struggle. Betsy is left on the ground

Frank (*aside*) Go on, Reuben. Hop it!

Reuben leaps away, in long jumps, with musical accompaniment. All boo! Reuben almost overdoes it—like a pantomime villain—pouncing on people

All (*singing*)　　Another attack by Spring Heeled Jack.
　　　　　　　　He could jump like this,
　　　　　　　　He could jump like that ...
Nelson (*excited as the Policeman*) At last we have a description of the rogue. By his latest victim, Miss Lucy Scales, aged eighteen, the sister of a Limehouse butcher. Miss Scales is blind.

Frank indicates to Zeldy to play the part

Young Jack (*aside*) How can she describe him if she's blind?
Frank (*aside*) He was the last thing she saw before she lost her sight.
Zeldy I was on my way home with my sister. We'd been at my brother's house. We went walking down Green Dragon Alley when suddenly this tall figure in a cloak jumped out of the shadows. He was wearing a kind of pelmet ...
Frank (*aside*) No, a helmet.
Zeldy Oh. A helmet, and a tight-fitting white costume like an oilskin. His face was hideous, his eyes were like balls of fire. Eyes of hell, they were. His hands had great claws. And he vomited blue and white flames. Some of the flames reached me as we struggled, and blinded me.
All (*singing*)　　With claws of steel
　　　　　　　　And eyes of fire,
　　　　　　　　He could jump as high as the old church spire.

Frank indicates to Maria to do her bit

Maria I saw him bounding up and down my street, leaping from cobbles to rooftop, rooftop to cobbles.

Music **Young Jack** What a load of cobblers!

The others shush him

Maria Up and down, up and down. Me and my neighbours cornered him ... but he just vanished into thin air.

All (*singing*)   All the police in London Town
                           They couldn't pin him down.

Nelson (*as Policeman*) Several of my fellow officers have reported being terrified by a man who darted out of the darkness to slap their faces with an icy hand. Sometimes he hid in the shadows and made frightening noises.

The children all make frightening noises behind Nelson's back. He reacts

Aaaaaaah!

Nelson runs off. All except Frank hum or "La la" the verse over Frank's last speech

Music   **No. 9A**

Frank The mystery of Spring Heeled Jack has never been solved. Was he a being from outer space? An escaped kangaroo? Or a young nobleman playing pranks? Or did the people of London all imagine him? Who knows?

The humming stops

Personally, as a historian, I find the whole story quite preposterous. I don't believe a word of it!

Suddenly he removes his outer clothing to reveal a white, tight-fitting costume, puts on a helmet, and leaps about, scaring the women, and roaring. Screams, laughter and shouts of "Get off!" Applause. Frank acknowledges the applause, then does another few leaps towards the children, speaking in rhythm

Music   **No. 10**

                Jack be nimble,
                Jack be quick,
                Jack spring over the chimney brick.

He arrives by the children

Boo!

The children laugh or scream. After a short pause ...

Jack It's not "chimbley brick", Frank. It's "candlestick".

Act I   19

No. 10A   Music

Children   Jack be nimble,
                      Jack be quick,
                      Jack *jump* over the *candlestick*!
Betsy Come on then, kids, let's do it. (*She puts her candle on the floor*)

No. 10B   Music

Music starts with occasional singing of the traditional rhyme driving the dance. Betsy is first to dance. She lifts up her skirt and balances from side to side, then jumps the candle. The others join in. All take turns, even old Jack. Young Jack does his as acrobatically as possible

Meanwhile, as the number builds, the others clap in rhythm or join in the choruses. General merriment. A few ad libs such as "Could be a bit dangerous that" and "That old candle could give you a nasty shock if you weren't careful", etc. At the end, all applaud and cheer

Jack Cor! That takes me back a bit. Last time I saw stepping like that was at me and my Lucy's wedding.
Nelson Here, Maria, give us that old song about the Gypsy Wedding—you know, the broom-dance one.
Rose Oh yeah! What d'you call it? Green Broom?
Maria Oh no, I couldn't. I haven't sung that for ages.
Zeldy Yeah! Go on, Mum, I've always liked that one.
Tom Come on, Ria!
Maria No! Me voice isn't what it was.
Nelson Rubbish! You could still make a few bob passing the hat round in *The Green Man* any night of the week.
Children (*banging*) Song! Song! Song!
Maria Oh, all right then! But you'll have to help me out if I forget the words.

It is suggested that "Jack" might be best played by Young Jack and the "Lady" by Zeldy

No. 11   Music

(*Singing*)	There once was a Romany lived down in Kent,
	And his trade, it was cutting of broom, green broom.
	His lazy son Jack, he lay flat on his back,
	And he snored in his bed until noon, till noon,
All	He snored in his bed until noon.
Maria	The old man came home and indoors he went,
	And he swore,
Old man	I'll set fire to the room, the room
	If you don't rise and go sharpen your knives,

Music		And go down to the woods to cut broom, green broom.
	All	Go down to the woods to cut broom.
	Maria	Young Jack, being sly, he got up by and by
		And went to the woods to cut broom, green broom,
		But the day it was warm,
	Jack	So I thought it no harm
		To rest for a while in the broom, green broom.
	All	To rest for a while in the broom.
	Maria	Jack woke with surprise when the sun left the skies,
		And ran to the town to cry,
	Jack	Broom, green broom.
	Maria	He hollered and bawled and so loudly did call,
	Jack	Pretty maids do you want any broom, green broom?
	All	Pretty maids, do you want any broom?
	Jack	I tell you they're good, just fetch'd from the wood,
		And ready for sweeping of rooms, of rooms
		Come handle my ware, for girls, I declare,
		You never had better green brooms, green brooms;
	All	You never had better green brooms.
	Maria	A lady, being sat in her chamber so high,
		She saw this young man with his broom, green broom;
		She called to her servant and thus to her said,
	Lady	Call in that young man with his broom, green broom.
	All	Call in that young man with his broom.
	Maria	Jack entered the kitchen, and then to the hall,
		And up to this fair lady's room, gay room.
		She smiled and she said,
	Lady	I've a mind to get wed;
		Could you marry a lady in bloom, in bloom?
	All	Could you marry a lady in bloom?
	Maria	Young Jack said,
	Jack	I could.
	Maria	And the lady cried, Good.
	Maria	And they left by the light of the moon, the moon;
		And then they went back to the broomcutting shack,
		And were married by jumping the broom, the broom,
	All	And were married by jumping the broom.

The music continues. Someone grabs a broom from by the wagon and throws it C in front of "Jack" and the "Lady". The children start shouting "A wedding, a wedding". "Jack" and the "Lady" play up to the situation. The "Lady" pulls a shawl over her head

No. 11A

With joined hands held up in front of them at chest level, they "process" to the broom and step over it with mock grace. The children break up a loaf from the table and shower the couple with bread (as confetti). "Jack" and the "Lady" turn and step back with a bit more vigour. The crowd start to clap slowly. "Jack" performs a low bow to the "Lady" and indicates that she should jump over the broom alone. She starts to step over the broom, in time to the clapping. At the end of the sixteen bar sequence, she stands back and offers the broom to "Jack"

No. 11B

Music starts and "Jack" does a broom dance to mounting applause and encouragement; four steps of sixteen bars

General talk as Reuben gets another broom and lays it head to head with the one on the floor. Then he pulls Betsy out and they perform a double broom dance to applause. Betsy drops out while Reuben is still dancing and "Jack" jumps back in and they try to out-do each other with more complex manoeuvres. Eventually just "Jack" is left; he finishes the dance by throwing the broom down with a flourish. Cheers. The company then sing a final verse of "Green Broom"

No. 11C

All So Jack, the young broom-squire, he married the maid,
And they danced by the light of the moon, the moon.
There was eating and drink and a kiss when you please,
That was better than cutting of broom, green broom
That was better than cutting of broom!

CURTAIN

ACT II

No. 12 Entr'acte

The Lights come up to reveal the children dancing and singing "Fish and Taters", while the adults are sitting around the table on which are the remains of a celebratory meal

No. 13

Children (*singing*)

    Ei! Ei! Ei! For the fish and taters,
    Ei! Ei! Ei! For the fish and cod;
    La di du duddle, du di du di,
    La di du duddle, du di day.

The song is repeated as necessary

The dance: two children hold a stick horizontally, one at each end. One of them, holding on to his or her end of the stick, begins a heel-and-toe step, with an occasional back-fling of the right foot, while revolving and circling round, singing the words and humming the bars between

The adults applaud the children, then return to their conversation round the table

Nelson You going down for the potato pulling this year, Reuben?

Reuben Well, Tom and I was thinking about it, but you know the trouble we have when the Woods and the Smiths get together.

Tom Yeah. And now that the Smiths have actually moved to that new permanent site right near Spalding, they'd have a whole gang around them. No fear, not for us this year.

Jack I remembers a time when the Woods and Smiths were the best of friends and it was the Boswells and Scamps didn't get on. Funny how things change, i'n' it? (*He smiles*) When I was a youngster whenever we got moved on we always asked the travellers on the road where the hell the Lees were—'cos we were sworn enemies in them days. Until old Amos Lees fell for our Nancy—silly sod! Spoiled our fun.

Nelson These kids today don't know what life on the road's really like. Lap of luxury it is for them.

Maria Mind you, I don't know why Dad keeps to his old-style wagon. You should have a new van, Dad, you really should. They do some lovely little trailers, all aluminium and fibre-glass with cut-glass windows.

Jack You'll be telling me to move to a permanent site next, Maria. The only fun I have nowadays is trying to stay one step ahead of the Old Bill. Ah, gone are the days when no-one came to move us.

Act II

23

The company sing

No. 14 Music

All	In the days before the motorways, When our horses had the time to graze, There were Coopers, Burtons, Lockes and Lees, And no-one came to move us.
Nelson **Maria**	We'd get some sticks and light a fire, And watch the golden flames grow higher;
Nelson **Maria** }	The Boswells, Brazils, Stanleys, Smiths,
Jack	The Coopers, Burtons, Lockes and Lees,
All	And no-one came to move us.
Rose **Tom**	We'd fill the kettle and make a brew, And settle down for a week or two;
Rose **Tom** }	The Patemans, Deightons, Chilcotts, Youngs,
Nelson **Maria** }	The Boswells, Brazils, Stanleys, Smiths,
Jack	The Coopers, Burtons, Lockes and Lees,
All	And no-one came to move us.
Betsy **Reuben**	The children watched the pudding boil, While at the hopping we did toil;
Betsy **Reuben** }	The Pinfolds, Prices, Woods and Grays,
Rose **Tom** }	The Patemans, Deightons, Chilcotts, Youngs,
Nelson **Maria** }	The Boswells, Brazils, Stanleys, Smiths,
Jack	The Coopers, Burtons, Lockes and Lees,
All	And no-one came to move us.
Nelson	We'd finish working in the fields, Then back to the camp for the evening meal; The Willetts, Drapers, Scamps and Shaws,
Betsy **Reuben** }	The Pinfolds, Prices, Woods and Grays,
Rose **Tom** }	The Patemans, Deightons, Chilcotts, Youngs,
Nelson **Maria** }	The Boswells, Brazils, Stanleys, Smiths,
Jack	The Coopers, Burtons, Lockes and Lees,
All	And no-one came to move us.

Music	Maria	We'd chicken, hare and rabbit stew,
		Pheasant, pigeon, hedgehog too;
		The Lovells, Herons, Hildings, Hughes,
	Nelson	The Willetts, Drapers, Scamps and Shaws,
	Betsy ⎱	
	Reuben ⎰	The Pinfolds, Prices, Woods and Grays,
	Rose ⎱	
	Tom ⎰	The Patemans, Deightons, Chilcotts, Youngs,
	Nelson ⎱	
	Maria ⎰	The Boswells, Brazils, Stanleys, Smiths,
	Jack	The Coopers, Burtons, Lockes and Lees,
	All	And no-one came to move us.

All take a deep breath and sing, speeding up to a very fast finish

> The Lovells, Herons, Hildings, Hughes,
> The Willetts, Drapers, Scamps and Shaws,
> The Pinfolds, Prices, Woods and Grays,
> The Patemans, Deightons, Chilcotts, Youngs,
> The Boswells, Brazils, Stanleys, Smiths,
> The Coopers, Burtons, Lockes and Lees,
> And no-one came to move us.

Cheering and laughter. All settle again, sitting round the fire

Tom You know, that's one thing I really couldn't eat, hedgehog.

Nelson Hotchi-witchi? Never eaten one? You don't know what you're missing! I keep trying to train old Bess to fetch 'em for me, but she won't have it. Will you, girl?

Jack Lovely meat, all pink, a bit like pork.

Nelson Maria does a lovely baked hotchi, don't you, gel?

Tom Nah! I don't fancy it.

Nelson You ought to try it. Cleaned out and stuffed with nuts and herbs and baked in clay on the fire—marvellous. You can smell 'em cooking half a mile away.

Jack I've tried everything. Blackbirds, greybirds, squirrels, hotchis ... but I wouldn't eat Badger ... there's too much bloody fat on 'em ... and, by Christ, they're tough!

Maria Here! D'you remember old Hapsy Smith? He was a bugger for finding hedgehogs. You could tell him a mile off, (*she laughs*) jumping up and down, trampling the brambles in the ditches with those great big boots of his. He could find hotchis' nests just by smell, I reckon.

Rose He looked like a hedgehog himself, didn't he? (*She laughs*) Those little beady eyes and his old brown clothes all wrinkled up.

Frank Sounds like Prickleback Jack.

Young Jack Who?

Frank Prickleback Jack. That story old Journey McDowell told. Remember, Grandad?

Jack Yeah. Full of stories, old Journey was.

Act II 25

Young Jack Well, I've never heard of Prickleback Jack.
Frank Must have been when you were in Kent for hop-picking. I had chicken-pox, remember? Had to stay here with Grandad. That's when old Journey told it. All the old 'uns sitting round the fire, just like now, and me under the wagon in the dark, listening.
Young Jack What was the story then?
Frank Well, Prickleback Jack was a Hedgehurst.
Young Jack A what?
Frank A Hedgehurst, a creature that's half-human and half-hedgehog.
Rose Just like Hapsy Smith.
Frank No. This was a creature who lived deep in the forest, feared by everyone.
Rose It *is* Hapsy Smith!
Frank Shut up!
Children Tell us it! Go on then! Please! (*Etc.*)
Frank All right, but you all have to learn the chorus and join in.

All react

It goes ... (*He sings*)

No. 15   Music

Jack, Jack,
Prickleback Jack,
Half-human and half-hedgehog.

He teaches it a couple of times, maybe including the audience

A guitar plays as preparations are made for a shadow mime, acted out behind the sheet on the line. It is suggested that Young Jack plays Prickleback Jack and Zeldy plays the Princess. Nelson or Tom could play the King, and Rose or Maria, the Nurse

The mime follows the action in the song, in simple dumb show and tableau, using basic props and costumes that will "read" in shadow

	The King went hunting one fine day, In the depths of the wood, he lost his way. He came to a hall and he knocked on the door, Then his blood ran cold at the sight he saw.
(*Speaking*)	For there stood
All (*singing*)	Jack, Jack, Prickleback Jack, Half-human and half-hedgehog.
Frank (*singing*)	Jack said, "I'll guide you home, O King, But in return I ask one thing. Whate'er it be that first you see When you get home—you must give to me."

Music		Now whenever he entered his castle grounds,
		The King was met by his faithful hounds.
		He knew they'd be the first he'd see
		So agreed to the bargain cheerfully
	(*speaking*)	With
	All (*singing*)	Jack, Jack,
		Prickleback Jack,
		Half-human and half-hedgehog.
	Frank	But the very first thing that did appear,
		Wasn't a hound, but his daughter dear,
		And then the King, he realized
		That she must be the hedgehurst's prize!
		And sure enough, when the hedgehurst came
		In a year and a day to make his claim,
		Though her father, he wept, and her mother cried,
		He demanded the girl was made the bride
	(*speaking*)	Of
	All (*singing*)	Jack, Jack
		Prickleback Jack,
		Half-human and half-hedgehog.
	Frank	When the moon, it rose o'er the castle wall,
		Jack led his princess from the hall;
		And he told her to lie on their marriage bed,
		"But I'll sleep down by the fire instead",
	(*speaking*)	Said
	All (*singing*)	Jack, Jack
		Prickleback Jack,
		Half-human and half-hedgehog.
	Frank	She went to her bed, but she could not sleep;
		At her monstrous husband she did peep.
		When the midnight chimes she faintly heard,
		Prickleback Jack woke up and stirred.
		He peeled off his skin and he let it fall;
		His back grew straight, he stood up tall,
		And he ran outside in the moonlight clear.
		But the Princess dared not move for fear
	(*speaking*)	Of
	All (*singing*)	Jack, Jack
		Prickleback Jack,
		Half-human and half-hedgehog.
	Frank	But at dawn he returned and the Princess saw
		Him don his hedgehog skin once more.
		She ran and she told her wise old Nurse,
		Who cried, "I fear 'tis a witch's curse.

Act II

	To break the spell you must burn his skin,	**Music**
	Then throw spring water over him."	
	So, next night when the Princess went to her bed	
	She was ready to do as her Nurse had said,	
(*speaking*)	To save	

All (*singing*)   Jack, Jack
Prickleback Jack,
Half-human and half-hedgehog.

Midnight starts to strike. Electronic sound effects rising in pitch to create tension. Jack peels off his skin, rolls it up and goes. The Princess picks up the skin and throws it on the fire. "Flames" rise

Frank   His skin in flames, she watched it burn,
And waited till dawn for Jack's return,
Then on him she threw spring water clear,
Crying, "Jack, I'll save you, have no fear".

Then Jack, he was freed from the witch's charms
And he took his Princess in his arms.
The rest of their lives was theirs to share
And that was the end of the strange affair
(*speaking*)   Of

All (*singing*)   Jack, Jack
Prickleback Jack,
Half-human and half-hedgehog.

Jack, Jack
Prickleback Jack,
Half-human and half-hedgehog.

All applaud Frank and the shadow mime actors

Suddenly Jason jumps forward and recites

Jason   Little Jack Horner sat in a corner
Eating his hedgehog pie.
He stuck in his thumb,
Right up its ——
And said, "What a good boy am I"!

All react with suppressed laughter or mock shock

Rose Come on now, Jason, that's very rude,. Especially in front of your grandad on his birthday, 'n' all. You must know better rhymes than that.
Charlotte I do! I do!
Rose All right then, love, let's hear you.

Jack picks up his fiddle and start to play for her; he accompanies the following nursery rhymes sung by the children

Music   **No. 16**

Children
Dik akai didakai
Jack has gone to poove the grye
Off the drom and into the tan
Five o'clock o' the rarti.

Charlotte (*announcing*) Jack and Jill.
  (*Singing*)
Jack and Jill went up the hill
To fetch a pail of water;
Jack fell down and broke his crown
And Jill came tumbling after.

Children
Dik akai didakai
Jack has gone to poove the grye
Off the drom and into the tan
Five o'clock o' the rarti.

Darren
Jack Spratt could eat no fat,
His wife would eat no lean oh!
And so between them both, you see,
They licked the platter clean oh!

Jason
Handy spandy Jack a Dandy
Loves plum cake and sugar candy;
He bought some at a grocer's shop
And out he came with a hop hop hop.

Charlotte
As I was going up the hill,
I met with Jack the Piper;
And the only tune that he could play
Was "Tie Your Garters Tighter".

I tied them once, I tied them twice,
I tied them three times over,
And the only song that he could sing
Was, "Carry Me Safe to Dover".

Children
Adults
Dik akai didakai
Jack has gone to poove the grye
Off the drom and into the tan
Five o'clock o' the rarti.

Jason
I'll tell you a story about Jackanory
And now my story's begun,

Darren
I'll tell you another of Jack and his brother

All three
And now my story is done.

The others applaud and cheer the children, who bow

Young Jack unobtrusively goes to prepare his "act", possibly behind the wagon

Rose I think we ought to thank Grandad, too—for playing for you.

Act II 29

All Hear hear! (*etc.*)
Betsy There's one rhyme you kids forgot.

Betsy mischievously sings to Jack, accompanied by Reuben, who "diddles" the tune as she sings the words

No. 16a   Music

(*Singing*)	Jack, come give me your fiddle
	If ever you mean to thrive.
Jack	Nay, I'll not give me fiddle
	To any man alive.
	If I should give me fiddle,
	They'll think that I'm gone mad,
	'Cos many's the joyful day
	Me fiddle and I have had.

Laughter and applause

(*Speaking*) All right, all right. Quieten down now. You've all done things for me. It's my turn to do something for you.

All cheer

I'll tell you all an old story about a fiddler.

All clap and sit, ready to listen

This is the story of Jack the Fiddler.

Applause

Many years ago, so the story goes, lived a young man called Jack the Fiddler. People called him that because he played the fiddle. He played it very well. But it wasn't an ordinary fiddle. It was a magic fiddle. For when he played it, everybody who heard the sound couldn't stop dancing. The music took control of their feet and they danced and they danced and they danced for as long as the fiddle played. One day Jack was walking through the woods. He'd been hunting, so he carried his gun and, of course, his fiddle, which he took with him wherever he went. Suddenly he saw a man coming towards him. He recognized the man as the local money lender. This man lent money to poor people in need. But in return he made them repay more money than he had lent them. The longer they took to repay, the more they had to repay. So much that many people ended up having to give him everything they owned. Jack didn't like the money lender because of his unfair dealings, and tried to avoid talking to him. But the money lender stopped him and said, "Hallo, young man, you look a bit shabby—why don't I lend you some money so that you can buy yourself a new coat?" And Jack said, "No thanks, I'm not interested in your money. I've heard how you fleece people and ruin them. I don't want anything to do with you." "Please yourself," said the money lender. "I'm only trying to be of help." Just then, a plump partridge went scurrying across the path in front of them and came to rest in a thornbush. "Did you see that?" asked the money lender. "The plumpest partridge I've ever seen. That would go down mighty well for my supper tonight." And seeing Jack's gun, he said, "Hey, lad, I might not be able to do *you* a favour, but maybe you could do *me* one." "Well," said Jack, "if it's within reason." And the money lender said, "Would you shoot me that partridge sitting in the bush, with that fine gun you've got?" "Very well," said Jack, and he put up his gun, aimed it at the partridge, and pulled the trigger. Bang! The partridge dropped down into the middle of the jagged bush. Thorns and briars all around it. Now, the money lender wanted the partridge for his supper. He wanted it so badly that he got down on his hands and knees and crawled into the middle of the prickly thorns to get it. And Jack suddenly thought to himself, "That money lender has cheated folk for a long, long time. I think I'll teach him a lesson." So he took his fiddle from off his back, picked up the bow and started to play, just as the money lender reached the centre of the bush. And when he heard the magic fiddle's music, he started to dance. He couldn't stop himself. Now, you imagine someone dancing in the middle of a thorn bush. The thorns pricked him and pulled on his clothes. And the faster Jack played the faster the money lender danced till his clothes were all ragged and torn and he was gasping, panting and didn't know what to do. He shouted out to Jack—"Stop, stop, stop your fiddling and I'll give you all my money. Please, stop!" "All right", said Jack, "I'll stop fiddling." And he did. And the money lender stopped dancing, crawled out of the bush, and gave Jack two bags of gold. Jack was very pleased with himself and set off on his way. But who should come by but a troop of the King's soldiers who were keeping law and order in the country in those days. They were like the police of today. If you had any complaints you went to the King's soldiers. And the money lender rushed up to them and said, "You see that man, he robbed me, look at the state I'm in, he tore my clothes and hit me and stole all my money." And the captain of the soldiers said, "Who would do such a thing to a poor old man like you? We must arrest him immediately." So the King's soldiers rode after Jack. "Halt!" they cried, and grabbed Jack, and took away the bags of gold, and the fiddle and the gun. So Jack was arrested and taken before the court. And the court found him guilty of robbing a man on the King's highway. He was sentenced to be hanged. Hanged by the neck until dead. They took the bags of gold and gave them back to the money lender, and locked Jack in the dungeons. Next day they built a scaffold out in the courtyard. In those days they built the scaffold in the open, so that everybody could come and watch the criminal being hanged. Jack was brought out and the huge crowd watched him climb the five steps up to the scaffold. The sheriff was there, all the councillors, and the ordinary citizens, men, women and children, even their dogs. Everyone had come to see Jack hanged. Including the money lender. The hangman put the rope round Jack's neck, and asked him, as was the custom, "What is your

Act II

last request? You can have one last request before you die." Jack thought for a moment, then said, "I would like to play my fiddle one last time." His request was granted. His fiddle was brought, and Jack started to play. **Music** And the moment he started to play, everybody started to dance. And the faster he played, the faster they danced. They danced and they danced and they danced. Everybody—even the dogs, and the pigeons perched on the rooftops—everybody couldn't stop dancing to the music of Jack's magic fiddle. Till the sheriff, panting with exhaustion, shouted—"Stop! Please stop." But Jack wouldn't stop. And everyone had to keep dancing. "If you stop your fiddling," shouted the sheriff, "I'll give you your life! I'll pardon you! You can go free!" Well, naturally, Jack stopped fiddling, and the hangman stopped dancing and took the rope off his neck. And everyone stopped dancing, and tried to get their breath back. And Jack pointed to the money lender, who had been dancing too and stood there panting like a dog in the heat, and he said, "Tell the people the truth, money lender, how you deceived them and made them pay you back more money than they should have done." And the money lender said, "All right, all right—if you don't play your fiddle any more, I'll give everyone their money back. And I'll give you a bag of gold, too." So all the folk who had been deceived got their money back. Jack got his pardon, plus a bag of gold, and the money lender was sent to the dungeons to pay for his crimes. And Jack went on his way and lived happily with his fiddle and his gun for the rest of his days.

All applaud and shout words of appreciation to Jack

Suddenly, from behind the wagon, the discordant sound of an electric guitar being tuned is heard

Jack What's that bloody awful din?
Rose Oh, it's our Jack getting ready to sing his song for you, Dad. He's quite good really, isn't he, Tom?
Tom Yeah. As long as you don't have to listen to him practise all the time! Christ, you'd think he didn't know you could turn the volume down!

Young Jack enters wearing a flashy jacket and his guitar. He positions his portable battery-operated amplifier speaker and prepares to sing

Cries of "Come on then, Elvis" and other suitable references

No. 18 Music

Young Jack (*singing*)
> You've heard him in the market
> With his saucy line of chat,
> He juggles piles of crockery
> And deals in this and that.
> Selling patent medicines
> That cure all known diseases,
> From chicken-pox and dandruff,
> Down to winter colds and sneezes.

Music

And as you watch him work the crowds
You've really got to smile,
For Jack's the lad that takes the cake
When it comes to style.

Chorus

He's Jack, Jack, Jack the lad,
A little bit of good and a little bit of bad.
Life's a game for rich and poor
And Jack's the lad who knows the score.

You've seen him at the fairground,
Going round and round and round;
Tattoos on his fingers
And his hair slicked down,
The lad who takes the money,
Gives your dodgem car a shove,
But he'd rather take your girlfriend
Down the tunnel of love.

Chorus

You've seen him in the local caff,
A punter by his side,
Selling him a Ford Capri,
It was his granny's pride:
"It's only had one owner, guv,
You know I've never lied!"
The punter coughs up half a grand
And is taken for a ride.

Chorus

You've seen him take his hat off
When he's stopped by the Bill,
"What me, sir? Well, I never!
Well, you see, I'm feeling ill.
I never touch a drop myself.
What! licence out of date?
I sent it down to Swansea,
Cor, the post's in such a state!
You never can rely upon
A single thing today,
With all the birds in trousers
And all the blokes turned gay!"
It's hard to earn an honest crust,
So he doesn't even try it.
He wheels and deals in anything
As long as mugs'll buy it.

Chorus

All applaud. Young Jack bows

Tom Not bad, son, not bad.
Nelson When's he going to get a proper job?
Tom Who knows? He's had the same chances as our Frank.
Betsy What are you going to do, Young Jack?
Young Jack Don't know, Cousin Bet.
Rose Well, you should be able to tell him, Betsy. You can read the future. Give her your palm, Jack.

Young Jack moves over to Betsy with his hand held out. She studies his palm

Jack Look! "Gypsy Rosa Lee"! (*He recites*)
> When I was a young man I held out my hand
> To a teller of fortunes, the best in the land
> She said in my palm all my future was there
> When I met her that summer at *Appleby Fair*.

No. 19   Music

The company freeze as the musical introduction to the "Appleby Fair" song starts. The lighting goes down on to Young Jack's palm. A glitterball effect covers the preparations for the "Appleby Fair" sequence

When the Lighting comes back up again, Betsy is holding a crystal ball. Young Jack looks in it. The company is still in a frozen position. Some of them might have had a small costume addition to suggest the change of location. Throughout the link into the "Appleby Fair" section, strange dreamlike noises, perhaps electronic, plus a sound effect of galloping horses, enhance the change of gear

All (*singing quietly*)
> There's gypsies from Hereford, Suffolk and Kent,
> Living in caravans, wagons and tents,
> They've piebalds and skewbalds and geldings and mares,
> They've come from all over to *Appleby Fair*.

Exciting drumbeats followed by a loud instrumental chorus, during which the company set the atmosphere of the fair. Fairground cries

> There's gypsies from Hereford, Suffolk and Kent,
> Living in caravans, wagons and tents,
> They've piebalds and skewbalds and geldings and mares,
> They've come from all over to Appleby Fair.

Nelson
> The farmers and dealers they argue and swear,
> A blacksmith beats up a new shoe for a mare,
> The lads run the ponies, the crowds stand and stare
> In the dust that's kicked up at Appleby Fair.

Music *Sound effect of horse hooves over the continuing music. Scattered, unconnected cries from the horse-dealers echo through*

Tom The old hag first, son...

Frank I'm washing her in the river; she's not ready...

Nelson Run Dobbin down the lanes then, lad. Show him off.

Reuben Pull his tail—make him look sprightly!

Nelson His bloody shoe's worked loose—slow him down! And keep them two stallions apart!

Tom Ride him bareback, lad! Hold his mane!

Reuben Mind that cart!

Nelson Come on, y' bugger, cheer him on! That'll make him prick 'is ears up!

The music ends as two horse-dealers meet. One leads in a hobby-horse to act as the Horse being discussed. Others gather and look on, encouraging or discouraging the buyer and seller, barracking and laughing

Dealer 1 Good-day, brother. I hear you might be on the look-out for an' horse. This brown one o' mine's got an 'eart like a lion... and lively with it.

Dealer 2 Good-day, brother. Lively? Your old brown 'un? I've seen livelier horses come out of a tin of dog meat!

Lady bystander Wore out, I reckon 'e is.

Dealer 1 Wore out? Dordi! Dordi! I reckon she must be going mad.

Bystander 2 Why, it's the kushtiest little grye you ever clapped yer yoks on!

Lady bystander A kushti grye? 'E reminds me of an 'orse I 'ad a couple 'o years back, and he was that nappie I 'ad to chop 'im in pretty quick.

Dealer 1 Work-shy? This 'orse'll pull till 'e drops.

Bystander 3 And that won't be long by the look of 'im.

Lady bystander Fit for the knackers, I reckon.

Dealer 1 Look, cousin, this 'orse is only three year old.

Dealer 2 'Ow old?

Dealer 1 Three year come Brough Hill Fair.

Bystander 3 Hey mush, I saw it *four* year ago when you was down at Barnet!

Dealer 1 Did I say three, brother? Sorry... I was mistook... I meant... um... five. But for a kushti 'orse as fit as this I couldn't take less than an... 'undred pound... that's if I was to sell it.

Dealer 2 An 'undred pound... (*he laughs*) ... brother you're a comic. I couldn't pay a penny more than... twenty pound—that's if I wanted a sway-backed nag!

Dealer 1 Sway-backed?

Bystander 3 And broken-winded.

Dealer 1 Oh brother, you surely don't know horse-flesh. (*He laughs and turns to the onlookers*) Sway-backed! Broken-winded. (*He shakes his head in despair*) I'll see you brother. (*He turns to leave*)

Dealer 2 Hang on, brother. I might be able to take him off your hands for ... thirty quid.

Act II

Dealer 1 I swear to God this horse is worth ... eighty pound to me if he's worth a penny. My chavvies love this grye, and they'd never forgive their old dad if I let him go for less than seventy pound.
Dealer 2 Forty quid!
Bystander 3 I'd take it, mush.
Dealer 1 Well go on then, *you* take it!
Bystander 3 Oh! My horse ain't for sale, brother!
Dealer 1 Sixty-five pound and that's it.
Dealer 2 Forty-five and it's a deal.
Dealer 1 Sixty and I'll throw in the bridle.
Dealer 2 Fifty.
Bystander 3 And throw in the cart.
Dealer 1 (*to Bystander 3*) I'll throw you in the bleedin' river! Fifty-five pound and I won't charge for a new set of shoes.
Dealer 2 Fifty pound and take 'em off.
Dealer 1 Fifty pound ... it's a deal.
Bystander 3 You've been done, brother!

Both spit on their palms and slap palms to seal the deal

Dealer 1 Kushti bok to you brother.

They slap their palms again

Dealer 2 And good luck to you too brother.

They slap their palms again

Dealer 1 We'll sort the money out down at the *Flying Horse*, shall we?

He punches Bystander 3 as they move away

All laugh and the general fairground atmosphere resumes

No. 19A Music

All (*singing*)	There's gypsies from Hereford, Suffolk and Kent,
	Living in caravans, wagon and tents,
	They've piebalds and skewbalds and geldings and mares;
	They've come from all over to Appleby Fair.

Fairground noises and cries

Women	The womenfolk meet and tell all that is new,
	The midwives address for a girl that is due,
	The children and dogs they can play without care,
	While the elders, they bargain at Appleby Fair.
Tom	With sinews of whipcord, and muscles of steel,
	There's tall men and small men all eager to peel;
	The cheers and the shouts they ring out through the air
	When they strip to go to it at Appleby Fair.

A fairground Barker calls to the crowd. A boxing ring is mimed to suggest a fairground boxing booth

Barker Roll up! Roll up! Come on, brothers, you all like a bit of sport now don't you! And here today you're going to see something of enormous proportions! Now calm down, missis! You all know Cast Iron Joe Betts; you all know Fighting Fred Price, who, incidentally, is due out next week; you all knew Harry the Bruiser, God rest his soul! Well, may my Uncle Tom be stone dead if I haven't found a fighter to beat 'em all. Ladies and Gents, I give you Gypsy Jack the Mighty Mauler.

Gypsy Jack comes forward and goes into various fighting poses. Cheers and jeers from the crowd

And to show my confidence in my boy, I've got this bag of golden sovs that I'll gladly give to anyone what can knock the Mauler down in three minutes!

Murmurs in the crowd

Come on, brothers, show your girls what you're made of. Wait a minute! Don't I see three of the Darlington boys lurking at the back? The very three what threw the copper through the window of the *Flying Horse* last Appleby Fair? Come on, boys and ...

Jack (Old Jack) pushes through the crowd

Jack I'll have a go.
Barker What?
Jack I'll have a go.
Barker No. Sorry, Grandad, this is a bit out of your league. Come on, you three, how about ——
Jack I'll have a go.
Barker Come off it, Grandad, we want a fight not a funeral. This boy's lethal. Come on, any offers?
Jack *(entering the "ring")* I'll have a go.

He quickly reveals long johns and vest and limbers up. Crowd laughter

Barker Oh, all right then, but don't say I didn't warn you! Now, brothers, in the circs. I don't mind taking a small side bet or two on this one.
Punter 1 Two quid on Gypsy Jack!

Barker collects the bets

Barker Two quid. Thank you, cousin. I swear I'm robbing myself. Any more?
Punter 2 A fiver on Jack!
Barker Right, brother, a fiver it is! May my Uncle Tom be stone dead if I don't lose my shirt on this fight!

He rings a bell. An amusing fight follows in which Gypsy Jack looks all-

Act II

powerful, but Jack nimbly avoids him and ends up landing one punch, which floors Gypsy Jack. Bell. Jack raises his arms, triumphant. Cheers and laughter. Boos from the punters. The Barker, concerned, rushes to intervene

Foul blow! You saw that, brothers! A karate chop! He's a black belt! My boy's orthodox! On your bike, Grandad!
Crowd Give him the money! Pay him! Boo! He won fair and square, *etc.*
Barker Oh, all right. The winner!

He gives Jack the purse. Jack leaves. Cheers

(*To Gypsy Jack*) Get up, you lily-livered yellow-belly!

Gypsy Jack tries to rise, but fails. The crowd wanders off, muttering. Suddenly Jack furtively returns and throws the purse to the Barker. Then he goes to Gypsy Jack

Jack All right, son?
Gypsy Jack (*getting up*) Fine, Dad!
Barker (*counting out the money*) Two for me, (*to Gypsy Jack*) two for you, and (*giving the rest to Jack*) three for Uncle Tom!

Gypsy Jack and Jack happily move away

(*To an imaginary crowd*) Roll up, roll up! ... *etc.*

No. 19B   Music

Music swells over his speech and the company return to the general fairground atmosphere

All	There's gypsies from Hereford, Suffolk and Kent,
	Living in caravans, wagons and tents,
	They've piebalds and skewbalds and geldings and mares,
	They've come from all over to Appleby Fair.

Fairground noise and cries

In the following verse, maybe one or two of the men perform a conjuring trick—sleight of hand

	There's silver-tongued tricksters and conmen and
Frank	thieves,
Reuben	There's wheelers and dealers could make you believe
Tom	That a broken-backed cob was a fine Arab mare,
Zeldy	So beware of a bargain at Appleby Fair.

No. 19C

Music. An actor enters on the hobby-horse. He recites a monologue in music-hall style

Actor	There was an old country farmer
	Who had an old black mare;
	Her mane was long and streaked with grey
	She looked the worse for wear;
	Her teeth were worn, her legs were tired
	Her tail was tied in knots;
	Her hooves were only good for glue
	But they wouldn't fit in the pots.
	He thought he'd take her to the fair
	And chop her for another;
	His daughter cried as he left the farm
	'Cos she loved that mare like a brother;
	When the farmer got into the town
	The horse he could not sell;
	Then some gypsies bought the bridle
	So he threw in the mare as well.
	They carried her to a local barn
	'Cos her legs was on the blink;
	Then they painted out the grey bits
	Till she looked quite in the pink;
	They filed her teeth and brushed them up
	With tins of Pepsodent;
	They clipped her mane and docked her tail
	They thought it time well spent.
	They took her back into the town
	And round the fair she sailed,
	Due mainly to the gypsies' whip
	And the ginger under her tail.
	They sold her to a dealer
	Who had had a drink too many,
	Then jumped on to a passing cart
	And fled to Letterkenny.

(*Aside*) That's in Ireland, madam!

> The dealer realized his mistake
> And sold her to a farmer;
> Then *he* jumped on another cart
> And fled to the Bahamas.
> The farmer proudly rode her home,
> His daughter heard him coming;
> "Our dad's brought back the old black mare,
> I can hear her hoofs a-drumming!"
>
> The moral of this story is
> You can't trust no-one these days;
> The horses that look spick and span
> Might really turn out resprays.

Act II

> With all your hard-earned money gone
> It would really make you blue
> To be the proud possessor of
> A walking pot of glue.

Nelson Rubbish! I 'eard it last year!

No. 19D — Music

Chord. Music hall "exit"

The Company reassemble, and recreate the fairground armosphere

No. 19E — Music

All
> There's gypsies from Hereford, Suffolk and Kent,
> Living in caravans, wagons and tents,
> They've piebalds and skewbalds and geldings and mares;
> They've come from all over to Appleby Fair.

Fairground noise and cries. Glitterball, to suggest a "return" to the gypsy encampment

During the following final verse, the scene changes back to where it started— i.e. Betsy looking at Young Jack's palm, and Jack on his steps. The verse is sung with reflective nostalgia for the good times

> They pack up their wagons with sadness and care,
> To travel the country, the devil knows where;
> The fields are all empty, the ground is all bare,
> Farewell to the site till next Appleby Fair.

Betsy looks at Young Jack's palm

Betsy I see you going on a long journey, Young Jack. Taking you far from these shores.
Nelson The farther the better!

Laughter

Betsy Something artistic ...
Frank Painting and decorating ...

Laughter

Betsy No, no, words ... learning ... but not learning like young Frank ... (*Suddenly*) I can see you ... on a stage ... acting ...
Tom Acting the goat!
Rose Tom! Don't knock him. He's good at theatricals. He's very good in the Jolly Jacks.

Music No. 20

Fanfare

Tom, Reuben and Nelson join up for cod opening to the Mumming Play, while struggling to get into their simple costumes

The Mumming Play is in the broad style of travelling players such as might be seen on village greens. The cast of characters (with suggested casting) is as follows: A Jolly Jack (Reuben), Jack Tar (Young Jack), the Hobby Horse, Little Egypt (Tom), Jack Ketch (Frank), and Doctor Myers (Nelson). The others become a participating audience, encouraging the real audience to join in, cheering and booing, etc.

Music No. 21

The chorus (*singing*) **(Nelson, Tom and Reuben)**	Good ladies and gentlemen, sat at your ease, Here come the Jolly Jacks eager to please! We've travelled Old England and honour we've won, There's no greater heroes with sword or with gun. Oh, the first of our Jacks that will enter the ring, Is a jolly Jack Tar who has fought for the king; He's a valiant young man and he's lately come back, So clear us a space and we'll welcome Young Jack.

Applause

Jack Tar I'm Jack the jolly sailorman, I've lately come from sea,
I've brought this poor old tatty horse to tramp the roads with me.
A Jolly Jack Say Jack, what sort of horse is that?
Jack Tar Why, it's a sea-horse, I tell no lies.
A Jolly Jack Why do you call it a sea-horse?
Jack Tar Because he's got two eyes.
One of them is deepest brown,
The other's brightest blue,
And I call him a sea-horse—
'Cos he can see as well as you.

He climbs on the horse's back and walks round in a circle singing

Music No. 22

"Here's Jolly Jack and his old horse", I hear the people cry,
The lads go shouting, "Whip him up" as I go riding by;

All shout "Whip him up"

Act II

		Music
	But I never use the whip because he trots along so fast,	
	Although his age is ninety-nine, he's game up to the last,	
	He's game up to the last!	

(*Speaking*)   Whoa, Ned! Slow down, slow down!
And let me catch my breath;
I swear if you keep up this pace
You'll run us both to death.

He climbs off the horse's back

> So here I am, your sailor bold,
> I've won ten thousand pounds in gold.
> 'Twas I that fought the fiery dragon
> And brought him to the slaughter,
> And by these means I won
> The King of Little Egypt's daughter.

Little Egypt (Tom) steps forward. He is dressed in women's clothes, with a beard

> I've travelled all the world around,
> But never a girl her equal found.
> Her father was the Pharoah,
> That's where she gets her hair-o;
> Her mother dressed in scarlet,
> That's why she's such a ... lovely girl.

Little Egypt   For me he slew the giant dead
And with that sword cut off his head.

Jack Ketch (Frank) rushes in and confronts Jack Tar and Little Egypt

Jack Ketch   What's that you said? Cut off his head?
Jack Tar just what's your little game?
I'm the headsman round these parts,
And Jack Ketch is my name.

Jack Tar   Not the hangman, Black Jack Ketch?

Jack Ketch   The very same, you little wretch;
I've got a heart as black as night
And I've nothing to do, so let's have a fight.
Come on, you saucy sailor,
Little Egypt, stand aside.

Little Egypt   Here, now don't you hurt my little Jack,
I'm soon to be his bride;
If you should kill my jolly tar,
I could never be his wife.

Jack Ketch	Then I'll do him a favour, And I'll try to take his life. My head is made of iron, My body's made of steel, My hands and feet are knucklebones; No man can make me yield.
Jack Tar	Oh, Black Jack Ketch, Don't speak in haste; If you fight with me Your life you'll waste; I'll hop you and chop you And slice you small as flies, And send you way across the seas To make mince pies.

Music   **No. 23**

All (*singing*)	Mince pies hot, Mince pies cold, Mince pies in the pot Nine days old. Some like it hot Some like it cold Some like it in the pot Nine days old.

This is repeated twice

Jack Tar and Jack Ketch set to and battle up and down the stage. Eventually, Jack Tar falls to the floor, dead

Little Egypt	Alas, alas, my Jack is slain, What must I do to raise him again? Here he lies in the presence of you all, I'll speedily for a doctor call. A doctor! A doctor! Five pounds for a doctor, *Ten* pounds for a good doctor, Is there not a doctor to be found To cure this deep and deadly wound?
Doctor	In come I, little Doctor Myers, I cure all my patients with a big pair of ... pliers.

He produces a large pair of pliers from a doctor's bag and shows them to the audience

Little Egypt	Doctor, Doctor, what is thy fee?
Doctor	Eight pounds ten, but twenty pounds to thee! How long has this man been dead?
Jack Ketch	Just half an hour since I cut off his head.

Act II

Doctor
Well, luckily I can cure all diseases,
Past, present, and to come,
Pimples on the elbow
And pimples on the ... thumb;
The cramp, the stitch,
The squitch, the itch,
The gout, the stones, the slag,
All with these pills from my little black bag.

He holds up some pills, which are brightly coloured rubber balls

Pains in his stomach,
Pains in his head;
Here now take this pill, sir,
This will raise you from the dead.

The Doctor pretends to give Jack Tar a large pill. The corpse sits up, then falls back, raising his legs. The Doctor pushes the legs down and his body lifts up like a see-saw

Jack Tar's behaving very funny;
I think the trouble's in his tummy.

The Doctor produces a large wooden saw and pretends to cut open Jack Tar's stomach. Inside he finds a long string of sausages

There's the trouble, that's what was wrong,
A string of sausages half a mile long.
Well, I've done the best that I can do,
And now I'm afraid it's up to you.
If you would have this noble youth
To rise up from the dead,
Give him three good hearty cheers
And raise him from his bed.
Hip hip hooray!
Hip hip hooray!
Hip hip hooray!

Jack Tar jumps up

Jack Tar
Once I was dead but now I'm alive,
God bless you all for helping me survive;
We're not the London actors
That act upon the stage,
But we're the Gypsy Jolly Jacks
Just trying to earn a wage.
And now our play is ended
And we have no more to say,
Give us all a hearty cheer
And we'll be on our way.

All Hooray!

All march round in a circle banging their swords together in rhythm

Music No. 24

The Jolly Jacks (*singing*)
> We're one two three Jolly Jacks,
> All in one mind,
> We've shown you our Mummers' Play;
> And we hope you'll prove kind,
> We hope you'll prove kind,
> With your money and strong beer;
> And we'll bring you some more luck
> The same time next year.

Applause and cheers as the Jolly Jacks bow, and remove their mumming costumes

Music No. 25

Music strikes up. Eight of the company (not Jack) dance an exciting eightsome reel. The audience is encouraged to join in, clapping in rhythm

All collapse; then, getting their breath back, start the rhyme "The Life that Jack Built", pointing out the different elements already used in the show. This rhyme can be divided up as required. It should build cumulatively

All (*except Jack*) This is the life that Jack built.

This is the wife that shared the life that Jack built.

This is the broom that married the wife
that shared the life that Jack built.

This is the wagon swept by the broom
that married the wife
that shared the life that Jack built.

This is the horse that Jack did groom
that pulled the wagon swept by the broom
that married the wife that shared the life that Jack built.

These are the children, both of whom
fed the horse that Jack did groom
that pulled the wagon swept by the broom
that married the wife that shared the life that Jack built.

This is the fiddle that played for the children,
both of whom fed the horse that Jack did groom
that pulled the wagon swept by the broom

that married the wife that shared the life that Jack built.

This is the tune that came from the fiddle
that played for the children, both of whom
fed the horse that Jack did groom
that pulled the wagon swept by the broom
that married the wife that shared the life that Jack built.

Jack takes the fiddle and plays one chorus of "Jack of All Trades". This leads to an exuberant chorus

No. 26   Music

All (*singing*)   He's a roving Jack of all trades,
Of every trade and all trades;
And if you want to know his name,
They call him Jack of all trades.

He's a roving Jack of all trades,
Of every trade and all trades;
And if you want to know his name,
They call him Jack of all trades.

All finish with a flourish, then turn to Jack

(*As a toast*) Jack the Lad!

Cheers and applause. Cries of "speech, speech!"

Jack I never knew such a wonderful day. God bless you all. I've worked hard all me life. Still do, come to that ...

The company make assenting noises, such as "Too bloody hard if you ask me", "Yes, it's true", "Grand old man"

But a day off now and then never hurts no-one. It's as my Lucy always said, "All work and no play makes Jack a dull boy." God rest her soul; I wish she could have been here today—she wouldn't half have been proud!

Silent pause

Well, come on now! Party's over! I'm not as young as I was and I needs me rest. Get along with you. Get the little chavvies home, it's past their bed time.

The company all give their individual farewells; kisses, handshakes, waves, etc., and exit

The stage is left empty except for Jack, who moves slowly, as if very tired now he's on his own. He sits on the steps of the wagon, elbows on his knees

God bless 'em. (*He rests his head on his hands*)

The Lights slowly dim

Jack exits

A spotlight fades up and focuses on the fiddle, hanging on the wagon wall. The rest of the stage stays dark

Music No. 27

A minor version of "Jack of all trades" is heard played on the fiddle. The spotlight slowly moves across the wagon to the steps, but Jack is no longer there

A second spot picks up Nelson as he enters and walks up to the wagon carrying a petrol can. He opens the wagon door and shakes some "petrol" in. He strikes a match, throws it in, and closes the door. He exits

Flames are seen to rise inside the wagon. The first spot continues its journey from the steps to the large box, which suddenly springs open. A puppet figure of Jack playing the fiddle pops up. A Jack in the Box. The music stops when the puppet is still

Black-out

CURTAIN

FURNITURE AND PROPERTY LIST

ACT I

On stage: Gypsy wagon. *On wall:* hook. *By it:* 2 brooms
Flat wagon
Table. *On it:* loaf of bread
Large box. *In it:* costumes and props as required for the various tales, including Union Jack **(Young Jack)**, spoons **(Nelson, Jack)**, sticks, candle **(Betsy)**
Washing line. *On it:* large sheet
Camp fire
Chairs

Off stage: Fiddle **(Jack)**
Gifts **(Company)**
Rucksack containing pages of script **(Frank)**

Personal: **Reuben:** hole stone on thong round neck

ACT II

Strike: Pieces of bread
Pages of script

Set: Remains of celebratory meal on table
Sticks for **Children**
Props and costumes for Act II including crystal ball **(Betsy)**, hobby-horse **(Dealer)**, bag of coins, bell **(Barker)**, bag containing pliers, pills, saw, string of sausages **(Doctor)**, puppet figure of Jack
Behind wagon: flashy jacket, guitar, portable battery-operated amplifier for **Young Jack**

Off stage: Petrol can, box of matches **(Nelson)**

LIGHTING PLOT

Property fittings required: camp fire, glitterball

Exterior. A gypsy encampment

ACT I. Evening

To open: General exterior lighting, camp fire effect on

No cues

ACT II. Evening

To open: General exterior lighting, camp fire effect on

Cue 1	During act *Gradually decrease lighting as night draws on*	(Page 22)
Cue 2	As preparations are made for shadow mime *Light behind sheet on line*	(Page 25)
Cue 3	At end of shadow mime *Cut light behind sheet*	(Page 27)
Cue 4	**Jack** (reciting): "… that summer at Appleby Fair." *Fade lighting down to* **Young Jack's** *palm; start glitterball effect*	(Page 33)
Cue 5	When ready for "Appleby Fair" sequence *Cut glitterball effect; increase lighting*	(Page 33)
Cue 6	Company reassemble, recreate fairground atmosphere and sing verse of "Appleby Fair" *Glitterball effect*	(Page 39)
Cue 7	When ready *Cut glitterball effect*	(Page 39)
Cue 8	**Jack:** "God bless 'em." (He puts his head on his hands) *Slowly dim lighting; bring up spot on fiddle, hanging on wagon wall; slowly move spot across wagon to steps*	(Page 45)
Cue 9	**Nelson** enters *Second follow spot on him*	(Page 46)
Cue 10	**Nelson** exits *Cut follow spot on him; bring up flame effect inside wagon; move first spot from steps to large box*	(Page 46)
Cue 11	When puppet is still; music stops *Black-out*	(Page 46)

EFFECTS PLOT

ACT I

No cues

ACT II

Cue 1	**Frank** (*singing*): "… as her Nurse had said. (*Speaking*) To save" *After chorus, midnight strikes, electronic sound effects, rising in pitch*	(Page 27)
Cue 2	**Princess** throws skin on fire *Fade electronic effects*	(Page 27)
Cue 3	During preparations for "Appleby Fair" section *Strange dreamlike noises, plus galloping horses*	(Page 33)
Cue 4	When ready *Fade dreamlike noises and galloping horses*	(Page 33)
Cue 5	**Nelson** (*singing*): "In the dust that's kicked up at Appleby Fair." *Horses hooves*	(Page 33)

www.ingramcontent.com/pod-product-compliance
Ingram Content Group UK Ltd.
Pitfield, Milton Keynes, MK11 3LW, UK
UKHW021901060225
454771UK00026B/403